You Too Were Once on Fire

Also by Peter E. Murphy

Books

A Tipsy Fairy Tale: A Coming of Age Memoir of Alcohol and Redemption

More Challenges for the Delusional: Peter Murphy's Prompts and the Writing They Inspired

Challenges for the Delusional: Peter Murphy's Prompts and the Poems They Inspired

Stubborn Child

Chapbooks

Looking for Thelma (Nonfiction)

Mean Time

The Man Who Never Was

Atlantic City Lives (with engravings by Michael McGarvey)

The Last Pub on Earth

I Thought I Was Going to Be Okay

Mr. Nobody

Thorough & Efficient

You Too Were Once on Fire

Peter E. Murphy

Terrapin Books

© 2025 by Peter E. Murphy
Printed in the United States of America.
All rights reserved.
No part of this book may be reproduced in any manner, except for brief quotations embodied in critical articles or reviews.

Terrapin Books
4 Midvale Avenue
West Caldwell, NJ 07006

www.terrapinbooks.com

ISBN: 978-1-947896-84-0
Library of Congress Control Number: 2025938650

First Edition

Cover art by

for Maxine Patroni

who taught me how to look at the stars
and hear their singing

Contents

The Diaspora of Light	3

I
The Book of Stars	7
The God Nobody Wanted	8
Death and the Miser	11
Glass Box	12
Prostitutes Appeal to Pope	13
Eclipse	14
Benediction	15
Rush Hour	16
Closing Time	18

II
The Hunger of Tides	21
The Fury of Bananas	22
Stairs to All Levels	23
Miss Besieged Sarajevo	25
Rahmat (Mercy)	26
Mulk (Dominion)	27
This Time	28
The Free Market	30
The Forgotten Man	32
House Angels	33

III
The Duality of Dust	37
The Business of Clouds	38

Restraint	39
In Wild Matrimony	40
Between Earth and Heaven	41
The Afterlife	42
On Pain and Desire	43
Hunger	44
The Payload	45

IV

Spontaneous Combustion	49
Art Song	50
Aspirin	51
Emergency Stars	52
Erased	54
The Resentment of Stars	55
Local Birds	56
Schooled	58

V

Home	65
Good Boy	67
New Tricks	69
Birthday	70
The Boy in the Tree	71
Bad History	73
Past Time	75
Grand Fugue	76
Stars Poetica	78

Acknowledgments	81
About the Author	85

The Diaspora of Light

When he saw it shooting from the eyes
of his students, Plato realized that, like imagination,
light must be restrained. So he tried to chain
it in a cave like the wild thing it is
and invented stories to explain the folly
of perception. This light has traveled far
to ignite us. And because it is always moving,
it cannot be held…or saved.
You might say its greatest strength
is that it knows it is dying. And when it does,
it breaks into a million colors.
Does it sadden you to learn that goldfish
see more of these colors than you do? Bees,
birds, lizards . . . they too see what you cannot see.

When we were one-celled and luminescent
in the pond that spawned us, there was no space
in our peculiar jelly for doubt to metastasize.
Why then, knowing our brilliance would fade,
did we abandon that world to walk upright?
Our folly was that we believed we would be happy
in exile, far from a homeland
to which we would never return.
Is it a strength for you? Or a weakness,
knowing that you will die? Is this why,
when light ebbs during the cooler months,
you find it difficult to lift your body
from your bed, and you cannot stem the tide
of water leaking from your eyes?

I

The Book of Stars

Although the sun is almost a perfect sphere
and more than a million earths can fit inside,
it is considered to be an ordinary star.
Does this disappoint you?
Were you hoping it was exceptional?
There may be more stars in the universe
than there are atoms on earth. About this
I'm not sure, but I'm certain there are more
stars than grains of sand or drops of water.
The light from these stars takes millions of years
to reach the earth. When you see this light,
imagine that you are looking at your own history.
Did you know *asterisk* means little star,
disaster, bad star?

The sun is middle-aged. Until the sixteenth
century it revolved around the earth, around us.
This means we were wrong.
It is a second-generation star.
This means much of the bright material
inside it, and inside ourselves, was once
part of a larger star that no longer exists.
This means that the sun, one day, and we also,
one day, will no longer exist.
Does this make you sad?
Were you hoping we would last forever?
Consider means to observe the stars,
desire, to await the stars.
What more would you like to know?

The God Nobody Wanted

The heart's ambition is to love.
That much is clear,
but what else?
Look at history.
Look at your own life,
how you have spent it,
what you own.
How has wealth changed you?
The ones you love?
What will it say on your tombstone
other than *consumer*?
Have you thought about altruism
in ants and wondered
when they will replace us?
Have you spent any time looking
for what you could not see,
like Galileo or Copernicus or Luther?
Do you know the Buddhists
have a sutra that foreshadows
the Sermon on the Mount?
Another, the Prodigal Son?
Have you heard of the Upanishads?
What religion were the Magi?
Where did your God go after Darwin,
after Einstein? All right, not after Einstein,
but after Auschwitz,
after Nagasaki.
Is he still there?

In which language does he speak to you?
Does he repronounce himself
in the *Book of Mormon?*
The Wall Street Journal?
Has he opened a dollar store
in a strip mall?
Or has he been replaced
by a technological imperative —
if it can be done, it must be done?
Maybe your god still listens to you
like a stethoscope to bad air.
Or maybe he's busy swapping DNA
in the protein of the colored bodies
of chromosomes. Perhaps placebo
surgery has left him recovering
in another century.
No matter what you say,
you are only talking about yourself.
And did you know the word *pontiff*
means bridge?
Linking what to what, I don't know,
as fathers stumble from parish to parish,
one kneeling boy to the next,
while forgiving each other's sins.
Is this what Meister Eckhart meant
when he wrote, "I pray God
to deliver me from God?"
That's about right.
In the end, we're food for worms
who have no higher aspiration
than to pass through the earth

as the earth passes through them.
An earth richer for their digestion,
beautiful, nurturing humus
on the other side.

Death and the Miser

—after Hieronymus Bosch

It's not the first time the dying man has ignored
his guardian angel who wants to slap him,
who wonders how he could reject eternal salvation
for a bagful of coins he'll never spend.

If the angel had been born in our world
instead of his own, he would understand
how flesh pulls stronger than a flap of wings.
Death points his arrow toward the expired heart,

and that's it for the miser. He's finished.
Doesn't matter to Death which way the soul goes.
He's just the driver—give him a cart and a corpse
and he's happy, will take it wherever the invoice says.

Then there's a priest at the foot of the bed.
One hand holds rosary beads, the other tosses coins
to a devil. If it weren't for these demons, the priest realizes,
he'd be out of work, just another poor slob hoeing

the rocky soil, eating slop, sleeping with livestock.
Instead he ministers to the souls of peasants,
tithes them, watches them die young,
consoles the bereaved with incense.

When he's through here, he'll return to the rectory,
have dinner sent in, some wine. He's pretty sure
nothing lives for eternity. Perhaps he'll teach
another set of conjugations to the new boy.

Glass Box

Unlike Galen who spliced ape into the shape
of human muscle, Vesalius cut apart the bodies
of the dead to show how different the human is.
He called his specimens muscle men, hung them
by the neck and shoulders from walls and posts,
then sketched them into imagined landscapes.
The illusion is that these landscapes are places
where his muscle men actually lived, not ink
engraved into paper to give the bodies depth.
Depth is also illusion, like the 3-dimensional sketch
of a glass box which appears to show its inside
and outside at the same time. When he couldn't
negotiate a corpse from the executioner, Vesalius
dug one up in the graveyard and hid it in his bed.
Of course, he got in trouble with the Church
when he proved men carried as many ribs as women
and argued against the "indestructible bone"
that would bear a new body at resurrection.
Returning from the Holy Land, Vesalius went down
in a shipwreck near the island of Zakynthos.
When his seven volume *Fabrica* of human anatomy
was published, some cleric threatened to hang him,
yelling, *Where is the soul?*

Prostitutes Appeal to Pope

Years before his name ascended from a Vatican chimney,
he sat in a dark booth as professional as the girls
who exposed their souls for him to absolve.
Occasionally he would ask, How many times?
Are you sorry? Is there anything else?
But mostly he sat, hands folded across his lap.

He preferred the girls to the gangsters who rattled off
their trespasses like statistics, and he despised the bureaucrats
who preached austerity to the masses then slinked in
each week for him to forgive them their excesses.

The girls, however, waited past absolution, sometimes
placing a cheek against the screen, sometimes asking how
he was, if there was anything he needed. Of course,
he said no, grateful for a calling that blessed his earthly
toil as he rose out of the darkness into the sanctified air.

Eclipse

I am looking at the moon.
It is a half moon
hazy
           and very amber.
Unlike the songs,
it doesn't do anything—
           no dancing with the stars

or turning into gold.
It doesn't spread green rumors
about itself.

It just hangs there
ignoring the equinox,
forgetting its meteorites
      and missing rock specimens.
The fact
        that I am driving
                over

the Throgs Neck Bridge
doesn't move it at all,
even when I am tided
into the fog, which swallows my sight,
and I am wrapped up in it.

Benediction

      It was the plane circling at Idlewild
unable to land, unable to stay aloft,
            that fell into the grace of Jamaica Bay.

      It was early evening. Spring. The Fifties.
It was a neighbor's blue station wagon. The noisy drive
            to the beach.

      It was the impressions we made in the wet sand.
The weeds. Remains of a bulkhead.
            It was the bird sanctuary across the bay

      on Broad Channel Island. A bridge. Traffic
to Rockaway. It was the sound of the engine.
            A prop. Its sick cough.

      It was a face in the window as it circled.
Too many faces. In church that Sunday, it was the way
            the Father described wading

      waist deep through the water, blessing
the parts of bodies. Blessing their souls. All that floated
            and sank. Bless them all.

Rush Hour

There are days when the dead seem to rise
out of the earth and die again on the road
in front of you when you're late for work.

Or worse, they give you the finger when you honk
them into the intersection
after the light has turned green.

The dead have no need for speed
or movement. Their catching-up days
are over. They only like going out

for a breath of air, a glimpse
of the horizon, and man, do they get pissed
when the commuter behind them becomes fidgety.

What are you rushing for, Asshole?
they would yell if they could. What's your hurry?
Dontcha know that where you think you're going

won't be there when you arrive?
The dead know things the living
ought to know to make life less miserable.

That happiness is good health and a bad memory,
that obscurity is forever, that tragedy
is when you get what you want.

Oh, if only it weren't wasted on the living,
they sigh to each other, as a cortege of traffic
piles up behind them.

Closing Time

The 24-hour bars in Atlantic City have three happy hours
a day, so I can pursue happiness whenever my shift lets out.
I know the end is near when the cleaners appear to scrape gum
from the gaudy carpets and drizzle disinfectant over urine
dripped from the dicers who don't want to lose their place
at the table. Gullible men who believe they can game the ivories
they toss across the green felt when they can't control their bladders.

I used to think life was a chain of dominoes, and if I tipped
one over, all my problems would come a-tumblin' down.
I also believed being happy was the key to happiness,
and that just made me sadder. Everyone suffers, my friends,
and most of us suffer more than others as we lumber
down the Boardwalk from *Pampers* to *Depends*,
mewling and puking and leaking at both ends.

II

The Hunger of Tides

DaVinci was convinced that the tide
was the breath of a beast he could not see.
You agree. It swamped your sandy house
in the super storm, washed your grandfather
up on the wrack line, pulled under
the heavy mood of the mother you barely knew
as she tried to stay afloat. Stay afloat.
You wish you were born part tide
and rise above these anxious seas.
I will take what you love, it sings,
pressing you to love so little, so little,
pressing you to rise and fall, rise and fall.
What the tide wants from you,
you do not want to give.

Galileo felt in its movement the movement
of the Earth, moving him to write
that the Earth is not the center of the Earth,
moving him to live under house arrest
until he died. When you dove
into the Mediterranean, it rocked you
against a crag that rose out of that wild sea
as if it too, needed to breathe. Breathe.
It opened your wounds to brine —
sinew, muscle, nerve, bone, memory —
and shame. The tide continued to roil
Galileo's imagination. Imprisoned in his home,
he looked at the stars for confirmation
until he went blind.

The Fury of Bananas

When these bright berries of the sun landed
on our shores, we could not pronounce their name,
so we called them *fruit of the wise men*.
Now they thrive in every superstore and bodega,
golden, ripe, inexpensive—ready to slice
on flakes of bran and corn.
Each is a clone of the other, their seeds
and imperfections bred out of them.
Does this surprise you?
Did you think God made them this perfect?

Chiquita taught us to sing *Bananas
have to ripen in a certain way*,
but she never sang to the men
who handled them, that the ripening
gases would unripen their seed,
causing a generation of their children
to never be born.
Does this upset you?
Did you not want to know this?

As you wrench a finger from its bunch,
as you bite into its flesh, imagine
you can hear the gunfire
that, according to Márquez, massacred thousands.
Would you prefer to ignore, for this sweetness,
a century of slaughter?
Will you ever ripen to the fact
that the poorest workers will always
never enjoy the fruits of their labor?

Stairs to All Levels

> *I'll sleep on the yoghurt*
> *and dream of the Persian Gulf*
> —Frank O'Hara, *Lunch Poems*

Today is Frank O'Hara
walking through New York
ignoring the news on Fox
and CNN, listening
instead to Rachmaninoff
and the Milky Way,
whispering in French,
tripping over the names
he dropped before Larry Rivers
eulogized him to the hordes
of mourners, each of whom
believed he was their best friend.

Today is Frank O'Hara
stepping away from them.
He will not scan headlines
for fallen stars, drop in for a beer
with Mike Goldberg,
nor listen for the click
of chorus girls, hard hats
and yellow cabs.
He does not recall headlights
blinding him on Fire Island.

Today is Frank O'Hara
walking through New York

as the Towers blossom and fall.
He cannot revise the terrible future
he conceived,
> *Where does the evil of the year go*
> > *when September takes New York*
> *and turns it into ozone stalagmites*

Oh Frank, I wander restless
through your corpus which joked
the future into consciousness.
Who would have known you
were serious as a bomb,
not arrogant when you wrote
> > *silent, listening to*

the air becoming no air becoming air again.

Miss Besieged Sarajevo

—May 1993

Imela Nogic, 17, blonde and shrapnel scarred, embraces
her runners-up and smiles a flare-bright smile.
Although she has won, she is afraid her boyfriend
will think her dirty for prancing in the swimsuit.
Although she has won, she is afraid.

Imela Nogic, 17, would love to compete for Miss World,
if only her boyfriend and her father would not object,
if only she could leave her city of snipers and shells.
She carries no flowers as she limps down the runway.
She unveils a banner, "Don't Let Them Kill Us!"

Imela Nogic, 17, says "Plans? I have no plans.
I may not even be alive tomorrow." Behind her,
judges sit with Uzis between their legs.
They have no talent to decide in Sarajevo, no evening gown.
No prize. The audience breaks into silence.

Rahmat (Mercy)

—for Olya Roohizadegan

When the inquisitor says you will be hungry,
you starve. When he says you will be cold,
you freeze. Today, you have been whipped.
He has taught you pain every day for a month,
and you have learned it.

He demands that you sign a paper.
When you refuse to renounce your faith,
he slaps your face and kicks out your chair.
His pen drops with you to the stone floor.
He screams, *Get up, you whore!*

You reach for his pen, gold, encrusted
with jewels—beautiful!
You offer it to him and you say,
I hope your pen writes the truth.
You say, *I will pray for you.*

The inquisitor lifts you to your feet,
drags you through the jaws of Sepah Prison
to your cell. *Sister,* he whispers,
will you pray for me, really? as blood seeps
from the soles of your feet.

Mulk (Dominion)

After her nails are ripped from the tips
of her fingers, her heart breaks loose from her body,
floats above the soldiers' heads and sings,
Bahá'u'lláh! Bahá'u'lláh!

They tell her to make the thing shut up,
but her heart continues to intone the name of her lord.
When one swings his club around to smash it,
her heart leaps to a higher note, and her song ricochets

off the walls that had heard so much and repeated nothing.
When the soldiers fail to silence the woman's heart,
they shout at the cage of her husband, *You get her to stop
or we'll kill you again.*

But the husband's eyes are closed, his lips stilled,
and when they kick his side, his heart bursts
forth and joins the heart of his wife singing,
Bahá'u'lláh! Bahá'u'lláh!

The soldiers take up their weapons and fire recklessly
which causes their shrieks to flow out from their bodies
into dark pools and coagulate on the soiled floor
of Adelabad prison.

This Time

Bombs are going off all over the city,
first this street, then that street, and soon,
I begin to think there are more bombs
than streets. This is how terror works.
It wants me to believe the man slicing
lamb in the kabob shop is planning
to slice me. It wants me to believe
thousands and thousands are cheering
on rooftops. Terror doesn't want me
to know I'm more likely to be crushed
by a truck as I walk home from work,
more likely to be shot by the gun
my wife keeps cocked under her pillow.
What I don't understand is how living
in this country makes me exceptional.
What I don't understand is how anyone
can say God tells them to kill.

I want to go to the ocean.
I want to forget everything I know.
I want the water to refresh my sweltering body.
I want to swim out to the salty horizon
and not let the waves roll me back to terra
firma where terrorists have tripwired the sand.
Listen, what I'm trying to say is,
Thank God they didn't think to blow up a church
in Birmingham or a federal building in Oklahoma.
Thank God they didn't think to blow up

the heartland, the salt of the earth, the middle
of this country that doesn't trust its coasts.
Thank God, they don't know how much
we already fear each other.

The Free Market

The Egg Lady gave birth to an egg.
The Chicken Lady gave birth to a chicken.
Because they worked in different parts
of the same industry, neither recalled

knowing the other. And, in case you're
wondering, it doesn't matter which came first.
What matters is that the young egg
and the young chicken became friends.

The egg wasn't good at getting around,
so the chicken carried it within her.
The chicken wasn't good at staying still,
so she sat on the egg and was calmed.

When the Shop Man gave birth to a shop,
he invited the chicken and the egg to move in.
Believe me, he said, You can trust me.
Believe me, he said, It's going to be great.

The Shop Man gave them space on a shelf
where the customers could see them.
Soon the chicken and the egg disappeared,
replaced by another chicken and another egg.

And on. And on.

Some people didn't notice.
Some people noticed and didn't mind.
Some people noticed and protested.

I don't know what the big deal is, said the Shop Man. I am running a business. I am a for-profit business. I am not hiding from that.

And that was that.

The Forgotten Man

The man who forgot himself rises
out of his cardboard sleep into the concrete morning
to relieve himself of hunger.
Everything has acquired use—trees have become lamp posts,
deer have turned into taxicabs that whistle down
Park Avenue on cloven tires of rain.

He walks among the citizens of this canyon
and sees himself reflected in plate glass, blurred
by blue buses, yellow livery, gray commuters
that dash across his own dim image in the shiny panes.

Eventually, when he recalls his faceless face upon well-fed
mannequins, his life loses sense. He sees himself in shop
window after shop window with his palms open to tokens and change,
open to a currency that will carry him through elements
that are benign, where the trains that rumble beneath
the surface wheeze silently all through the screaming night.

House Angels

    Smoke circles the roof like a dark halo.
Inside the house a fire rages. When I enter,
        a man is sitting down to dinner.

    The people who live here, I ask, where are they?
I am about to eat them, he says, won't you
        join me? They are so delicious when fresh

    and I have plenty. I couldn't, I say,
I am too fond of those people.
        No, these are not your people, he says.

    They're mine. Please try one.
Those look like my pajamas you're wearing, I say.
        And isn't that my coffee mug?

    He shrugs his shoulders and digs in,
placing a napkin on his lap.
        I leave the house I thought

    was mine and wander through the neighborhood
that is less and less familiar,
        intruding on men who consume their families,

    looking for the right house with the right people,
where the children I left on the fire
        are more than ready.

III

The Duality of Dust

Although its name means *tiny*, dust flashes
in the veins of comets like celestial corpuscles,
builds rings around Saturn, makes up the flesh
of stars sucked into their negative darkness,
and again when they burst back into flame.
You wonder how many times, how many times
a thing can be born, as it fashions star after star,
each one bright and sizzling, *trailing clouds of glory*
in its wake. A *genuine birth*, as Wordsworth said
of poetry, *a bursting forth of genius from the dust*.
You wonder what it understands about your tiny
planet that seems so large to you, you believe
that it *is* large. You wonder why you understand
so little about everything.

Like us, dust is worn from traveling.
As it swirls across the Atlantic from the Sahara,
instead of brightening, it darkens the sky.
Some call the winds that carry it, *Haboob,
Khamsin, Simón, Sirocco*. But when you name
a thing like that, you risk giving it a soul.
Gandhi said that the seeker after truth
must be humbler than the dust, but you
are dogged by an ego so fierce, it sucks you
into its own black hole. And you have become
so full of desire, so full of desire, it tears
at your flesh. When you reach for your beloved,
it's as if she is of the firmament, passing, like a breeze,
between your outstretched arms.

The Business of Clouds

Of all the tribes of the firmament, they are the hardest
working, as they tug ton after ton of vapor from one sky
to another. Sometimes you bless them for tinting
our ceiling so prismatic your breath gushes
from your body. But mostly you ignore them
as they cast your day into a day of shadow.
Milton gave his a silver lining to console himself
when he went blind. And Wordsworth called them
lonely as he walked alone on Windemere's shore
that breezy morn. Like our kind, they are born. They die.
But unlike us they reform unhemmed by time and desire.
We have always aspired to be like them.
Think of Icarus, *tossing his head in sprightly dance*,
before falling, like rain, from the sky.

As you recall Dickinson's last words, you begin
to feel the damp body of fog touching you where you
do not wish to be touched. No, not from the sky,
it has risen out of the earth, out of the earth,
hauling the heaviness of the earth with it.
I must go in, she said, choking on the weight
of the air, *the fog is rising.* No, not on *little cat feet,*
but on the claws of a beast that crushed the breath
out of her body. Now all your desire wicks away
except your desire to arrive where you meant
to arrive when you meant to arrive there.
You trudge along, trudge along, your face facing
the ground you can hardly see, instead of looking
upward where the sun ought to be.

Restraint

Dagwood kisses Blondie goodbye and leaves
early avoiding his daily run-in with the mailman.
He is usually driven, but today he releases
his carpool to its daily jam and walks to work.
Since the heart attack, he's been exercising—
really, he's fine!—although they haven't slept
together since he left the ICU and she moved
into the guest room.
The osso buco was awful last night.
How could she forget to add the wine?
He wanted to say something, but she seemed distracted.
And when he went down for his midnight snack,
they were out of prosciutto and the focaccia was stale.
Maybe she has a lover?
Herb, a recluse since Tootsie died?
Young Elmo back from the war,
uncommunicative, but deadly handsome?
Who else could she be dithering with?
Maybe it's her change of life? When he asked
if she still gets her period, she slapped him.
He was easy to please, but he knew he was boring.
When he brought up the election at breakfast,
she said, Who cares? Nothing ever changes.
And even though he agrees, it was one
of their favorite topics, drinking
their fair trade coffee, reading the *Times*.

In Wild Matrimony

The marriage has broken loose—
its people had been feeding and lodging it so long
they didn't notice the beast it had become.
They grew oblivious to its fury,
its disdain for the processed oats they fed it
until it nipped at the bride, refused
to just stand there when the groom approached
with his brush and a handful of clippers.

Worse, they mocked it, wore their suit of matrimony
like a vaudeville horse, she trotting in front,
he stuffed into the hind quarters.
And when they danced about so gracefully,
who could blame them for thinking the thing was tame,
even as it rose on its back legs to kick the guts
out of their small house?

How pathetic they looked after they bolted the doors—
two adults stumbling through the neighborhood
waving the thin ends of their rope like a lasso.
Each wears the frayed half of a costume
which has fallen around their knees.
First the ass, then the head, screams at the other,
Come back, I'm warning you. Come back!
as they trudge past the intersection of Walk
and Don't Walk, head on into the wedlocked traffic.

Between Earth and Heaven

      She was blissful at the eclipse party,
said they should celebrate as she danced across the lawn.
            It all reminded him of his marriage,

how sorrow consumes joy like a turtle
            eating its own eggs. Watch how fast I twirl,
      she laughed, spilling red wine on her wine-red dress.

            How quickly things seep into their own darkness.
How deeply sweetness is absorbed by its shadow.
      Come dance with me you love-sick fool, she sang.

      Let's celebrate our moon affair. Let's celebrate
            our desire. And after, he realizes, how hard it is
to see in this light. How much it hurts the eyes.

The Afterlife

Walking on the beach this morning I saw a rocket boost a shuttle
from Canaveral, not straight as I had expected, but off on a curve.

The higher it climbed, the more it curved.

Now there's a storm that sounds like women screaming,
and a dog chained on the beach barks to chase it away.

There are a billion things living in this ocean
and I am not conversant about any of them.

The last thing she said, she said your carnival season
is ending, and all you can do is lie about it.

On Pain and Desire

I am happy I've learned to not always eat what's good for me.
So when I crave something salty, I bite into the red heart
of an olive or suck the tears of anchovies I've stuffed
between two wings of bread.

And when I read how Boethius, in prison, brings Philosophy
to climax, while Ovid screams unfair from his erotic exile,
I think I'm beginning to understand life's subtlety.

I used to believe a tyrant programs our desire
to cause us pain. But now, I am sure, it is an idiot savant
expressing his inarticulate genius,
trying to make us happy so we will love him in return.

Hunger

I picked the locks mother chained
around the refrigerator.

She hoped steel could keep me
from its gleaming eggs, their golden hearts.

I remember my first cake,
my first coffee, first steak.

I remember biting into mother's breast
until she screamed.

Outside the kitchen window
black birds flutter the branches.

Their noises fly
past my open mouth.

How many baked into a pie?
Come here my darlings.

Your wings are feather and bone.
I only want to swallow your song.

The Payload

I am going off all the time, even when I sleep
or try to stay asleep. Bombs from the horizon
of my dream rip into my head, detonate
their drone until there's nothing but fire and noise.

Lying in bed as my own engines rev,
I nauseate from the sweat of machinery.
My legs bounce so hard they shake
my wife out of her sleep night after night.

My hands lurch above my pillow, smack into glass.
I hear the hiss of acetylene torches weld
the cockpit locked around me. I plunge through air
toward the cruiser that grows too large, too quickly.

The last thought I have before going off is where to strike it.
You must decide which way it's going to be, the shrink tells me
after another false cardiac arrest. This time the head, Big Guy.
Next time the heart.

IV

Spontaneous Combustion

It was an ordinary day at work, he thought,
when he felt the first thump in his chest.
He paused, as if hit with the tip of a pointer or a cane.
Excuse me, it said, and he gave it his attention.
What now? What do you want?
Don't worry, it replied. I'll make it quick.
And it did, exploding throughout his chest,
making it a chest of fire, a whole house of fire,
burning the oxygen out of his lungs.
No, he shouted. Not now! Not now!
but it said nothing. It didn't need to speak.
It had no need for words of any kind.
No, No, he thought he said, but he hadn't.
He just lay there ablaze, giving in.
He wanted to say, All right, you said
you'd make it quick.
But he didn't say that either.

Art Song

He hears it when stopped in traffic
at the intersection where expressionless
commuters drift by behind winds of glass.

It's not the kind of music he could dance to,
nor would he dance if it were not for women
who think his soul generous.

No, he hears the music of insistence.
It's refrain—ME ME ME—is also the coda.
In between are stanzas of desire—ME you ME you—

until the light changes and he shifts himself
into drive, confused by the determination
of traffic revving its engines and the wipers singing

their little hearts out, brush strokes
on a snare drum, which is what he imagines
is the music of his own heart: a thin layer

of skin stretched over a hollowed root,
rattled by the swish and whisk of light fingers—
the scratch and fizz of air gasping through dry chambers.

Aspirin

I swallowed a handful after a pitcher
of beer did not get me high enough. Maybe
that's why I fell, swinging at a softball,
into a manhole in Central Park.
The pitch was sweet as I stepped into it.
The metal lid we called home was wobbly
after a player who climbed down, climbed back
up relieved, having taken a piss.
Because I wanted to be somebody,
I tried things I knew I couldn't do.
I swung. I missed. I fell into a hole.
Gravity pulled me like a planet, like a plant.
I take a low dose each night to thin my blood.
My clogged heart troubles me; it's still aspiring.

Emergency Stars

They never appear in the firmament
no matter how often you call for them.
You are running out of time, but time,
according to Einstein, is an illusion.
This means as your bones turn to dust in the wooden box
they are forming in your mother's womb.
This means you're both dead *and* alive.
Einstein imagines shooting a twin into space
at lightspeed, and when it falls back to earth,
it's younger than the sibling it left behind.
This somehow proves he's right, but you can't reason out
why these stars don't come when you call them.
Like you, they must be fettered by gravity and doubt.
Like you, they must flail forever through the darkness.

Because you are a child living in hell, you think
you must be dead. What you pray for is someday to be alive.
That's why you look toward the sky, the way Descartes
looks toward the sky—*Hope is the desire of the soul
that the dream will come true.*
Your dream is for a mother's love.
But as hope suckled you from the teat of sour milk,
she too turned out to be an illusion.
Show yourselves, anxious stars. Damn it!
Show yourselves.
Screw Einstein!

You're running out of time.
Screw Descartes!
How do you prove to yourself that you are alive?

Erased

I fell in a manhole in Central Park and woke up in a gutter in Wales.
I didn't know there was a manhole in Central Park.
But because it was a manhole, I believed I was a man.

A man left Wales to build a city in Ukraine and gave it his name.
After the Revolution Hughesovka became Stalino.
After Khrushchev Stalino became Donetsk.

In Ohio a boy shot a BB gun at the last passenger pigeon.
In Ukraine a man shot a rocket at a passenger plane.
Every falling thing leaves a hole in the sky.

A man left a hole in his family when he left his family in Wales.
My mother believed that man was her father.
Born in shame, she never knew her real name.

My mother fell into a hole she could not climb out of.
Why does she still appear in my sober-sweet dreams?
Why do I believe she will say something that will change my life?

Someone airbrushed Wales off the official European map.
Instead of a hole, a bloated Irish Sea . . .

                      . . . where Wales ought to be.

The Resentment of Stars

If fire were stolen by a god who is tortured
for saving us, then this is what it must mean to love.
But no, it's just a bit of star that will never forgive us
for pulling it out of the sky. This is why fire snaps
at our fingers when we try to hold it. This is why
it will never love us, even though ours
is the only atmosphere in which it can breathe.
And why should it? How have we ever employed it,
but to build and destroy . . . build and destroy?
When you were a child you didn't see the flame
on the silver object of your desire, so you grasped
what you should never have grasped, thinking
it would please you. Instead, discharge from your
blistering palm soiled your father's handkerchief.

Betrayal has taught you how to live on molten
rock that's covered mostly by ocean, taught you
what a fragile engine the body is, taught you
to trust no person, no thing, no matter how bright
and gleaming. Forget the virtuous martyrs
whose blood soiled the fabric of your imagination.
Forget those saints crucified upside down, their skulls
cracked open by axes, their hearts cleaved from
their bodies, their bodies set ablaze. And that giver
of flame? Forget him too. Each day his liver
is clawed out by talons dispatched by those
who once loved him. And you, when you were young
and virtuous . . . young and virtuous, even then,
how could you ever doubt that the Earth is on fire?

Local Birds

Walking on the beach near Bodega Bay, I came
across a gang of turkey vultures looking me
over as they gorged themselves on the carcass
of a sea lion. I'd never seen birds like this.
They didn't sing or whistle or hang out on phone
wires. And they didn't scare easily, hissing
as I stopped to watch them devour the eyes.
If one had pulled out a pack of Luckys and lit up,
I wouldn't have been surprised. That evening,
they circled above me as I lounged in the Jacuzzi.
I flapped my arms so they wouldn't mistake me
for another dead seal. Then I went inside, put
on *The Birds* filmed here 50 years ago, and kept
my eye on the blonde, Tippi Hedren. Smitten
when he saw her in a beer commercial, Hitchcock
trained her to act terrified, tying a live crow to her
collar in one scene, and in another, sliding a wooden
gull down a wire at her face. Tippi got frazzled
and wound up in the hospital. In the film,
the locals blame her for bringing this horror show
to their quiet village. There's this smarty-pants
amateur ornithologist, a frumpy woman,
who snarls at beautiful Tippi. "I have never known
birds of different species to flock together."
On the beach the next morning I saw crows finish
off the last of that seal while the vultures stood around
looking like extras. Most of the buildings in the movie
are gone, but the restaurant is still there.

The owner back then, a guy named Mitch, offered
Hitchcock the place for free if the town in the film
be called Bodega Bay and the lead be named "Mitch."
He even snagged a speaking part. His immortal words
to Rod Taylor, "What happened, Mitch?"
I don't know how old she is or where she lives,
but Tippi returns to the restaurant each year
to sign autographs. I looked around one night
but didn't see her. At the Tube stop in London
near where Hitchcock was born, they put up mosaics
based on his films—Janet Leigh soaps it up
in the shower. Jimmy Stewart and Grace Kelly
stare out a window. Stewart again and Kim Novak
wrestle in a bell tower. Bob Cummings wears handcuffs
as another blonde, I don't know this one, drives
a getaway car. And there's our Tippi, screaming
as she runs from the darkness that swarms her,
raising her ceramic arms to cover her golden head.

Schooled

Well Rounded

>At first your skull
>is as soft as marrow
>coursing the currents
>of the birth canal
>which squeezes
>you between
>its narrow walls
>toward light
>and drops you
>into a stiff desk
>bolted to the wood
>floor by a catechism
>of wimples and robes
>which darken
>the gleam that tries
>to fill your head
>so that nothing
>anyone tells you
>after that nothing
>can make you
>not question it.

Transportation

>Half the fun
>is dallying

at the intersection
of Bus A and Bus B
getting off one
and not on the other
until the skinny hand
of the clock slaps
the last minute
the way the geography
teacher slaps your face
when you arrive
too late to recross
the river that flows
from his lecture notes.
How that lesson
repeats itself
demanding you keep
those barbarians
away as you figure out
how to beat them back.

Discipline

You are its
diligent follower
who believes everything
it teaches is smart
literally a disciple
whose hands
are stigmatized
by what they refuse
to reach for.

The more your palms
bleed, the less they feel
the more brittle
becomes the skull
pedestaled upon
your neck
so when you
finally stretch
you crack so bad
all the king's
losses are not able
to make amends.

Homework

    In language
    it is a sentence
    hanging above you.
    In math numbers
    that refuse to negate
    themselves until
    you reduce eternity
    to a few scratches
    on white lined paper
    the slippery shell
    of the fountain
    pen splots your loose
    leaves with blueblack ink
    as you compose
    the themes of the rest
    of your life

the sharp blade
of the deadline
free falling toward
the rigid skin
on the back of your neck.

Education

Most of it you get
after you leave
books and bricks
so when you're
finally tested
nothing you
studied does
you any good.
You're smart
because you cheat
on every exam
you take invent
stories to explain
the lessons you cut.
Now that your ass
is on the line
the only correct
answer is the one
that gets the job
done fast done right
and under budget.

V

Home

When I walked home from school differently
from the way I'd gone, I crossed my invisible wires
so badly I had to go back to untangle myself.
I retouched every fence post twice, every leaf
that got in my way, hoping to avoid the stray
that attacked me most days. I washed my hands
a lot, tapped my fingers and my toes, counted
things, upset when they were off.
When my parents yelled, Stop it! my smart mouth
yelled back, Stop what? earning it the slap.
They put me in a home for defective children
where I watched films of normal kids
making beds, polishing their shoes, putting them
on the right feet. I was made to pee in public,
take showers with other boys, clean bathrooms.
Once a day they lectured us on sin and what happens
when we let it in. I couldn't concentrate, fell behind
and flunked out. When I arrived home, my parents
slammed the door. Neighbors didn't open theirs.
Aunts, uncles claimed not to be related.
I sat on the curb in front of a museum,
my possessions tied in a bindle dangling from a stick.
I was no-strings-attached, just twitching arms and legs.
Would you like to come in? a curator asked,
and showed me to a diorama in the Family Wing.
Eventually I settled into a routine, grew up, got a job
counting things in a repository, married a restorer
from the American Collection. Our children crisscross

the neighborhood touching anything they like
or nothing at all. They play with other kids,
do well at school, pet dogs and hug my legs
when I walk home the same course each night from work.

Good Boy

I didn't notice the dog
until it barked, and I ran
to it so it could lick
my fingers, my face.
In the fields it taught me
a thousand scents that made
me dizzy. We dug holes,
chased other dogs, peed
everywhere, and resting,
it whispered, There, there,
my head rising and falling
on its chest, rising and falling.
Some boys need a mother,
a father, a bed, some toys,
none of them as happy as me
with the food we caught,
a puddle of water, a place
to lie down in the shade.
Remember yesterday?
I asked. Yesterday?
it repeated, dozing off.

One day a man strolled
into the field and whistled.
The dog fixed its eyes
on the stick in his hand
and took off, not caring
if it would beat him

or be tossed to fetch.
I too wanted the man
to throw the stick
for me to chase over
and over again, scratch
my ear and say, Good boy.
But when he strapped
a collar to the dog's neck
and attached a leash,
leading it out of the field,
my boy heart broke
into a howl and I stood,
for the first time, on my own
two feet, and walked away,
burying my wilderness within me.

New Tricks

When I took her into my home,
I invested in food, gave her water, and kept the yard
free of her waste. My house was full of everything
she loved. There was no need for anyone else.

But she wanted more.

She pawed at the door. So I sang to her. I sang,
Put on your cute little sweater, your doggy gloves
and galoshes, your slicker and your mackintosh.
We're going for a walk.

And, my friends, the bitch ran away.

I found her copulating in the cemetery
with a terrier named Toby.
I took her to get fixed
and while she was under, had her microchipped.

You understand, don't you?

Now, she mopes in and out of the living rooms,
forsaking my bed where she always slept.
She has grown so silent and restless, more like a ghost
than a dog. Most of the time I forget she is there.

Birthday

Once upon a time I lived inside a woman,
but when I started to drown I swam to shore,
and climbed out of her body, making us both cry.
She taught me to call her *Mother* as I tottered
from one place in the living room to another,
reaching for the silver tea set, cutting open
my chin on the corner of a coffee table.
And then she went away.
Maybe she pricked her finger on a needle.
Maybe she bit into a poisoned apple.
Maybe the knife she held while slicing it
slipped into her heart.
The last time I saw her I said, *Goodbye forever
in case I don't see you again.*
I had a picture or two in the wallet the mugger took.
She wore a white gown standing next to a dark man
in a dark suit. Was his name Father?
Now I am living inside a new family.
I suck air into my lungs and blow slowly
over the flare of candles until they go out.
I eat the cake they cut for me. They are terribly nice.
Happy birthday, they sing. Happy Birthday.

The Boy in the Tree

A boy flying his kite gets caught in a tree.
He doesn't like it, but the tree won't let him down.
His friends throw sticks and stones trying
to make an opening big enough for him to fall through.
His mother comes in an apron and tears,
and the boy screams that he's sorry for playing
so close to this tree they've had trouble with before.
His father returns from work
and demands that the boy listen to reason,
threatening him, withholding all of his allowance.
The mother begs the tree to give back her son,
offering it water and manure and sunshine.
The boy looks down at his family and his friends,
all the curious world of his puny neighborhood,
and he starts to cry.

The tree hadn't thought much of little boys
with kites, but his tears are so delicious and cool
sinking into the garden of its roots, it decides to keep him.
Eventually, the tree falls in love with the boy breathing
in its limbs and covers him with leaves, flowers and fruit.
The father begins cutting it back in the evenings
after supper, and on weekends after mowing the lawn
which has also begun to act up.
It takes years to make the tree manageable,
to prune it so it fits into a pot he takes into his house.
The father trains the tree, trimming it
back with scissors, placing weights on its thin branches.

And the little boy has also grown
smaller in this tree that loves him,
dreaming of kite tails and strong winds.

Bad History

I climb the steps to the High Line
at 34th Street and walk downtown.
Before it became an elevated park,
freight cars hauled dead animals
from the Meatpacking District
to Hell's Kitchen. When I was a kid,
before my mother did what she did,
I stood outside Kenney's Bar and Grill
on 19th Street and watched the parade
of bootblack engines lug car after car
of carcasses uptown. Now, tourists trample
the wildflowers while posing for selfies
they post on Insta-Insta.

I walk past a homeless guy holding a sign,
I could use some help.
Next to him an evangelist holds a sign,
Turn to Jesus for Help.
This is how the world is. Always has been.
My mother could have used some help,
but when she turned to Jesus he answered
in Latin. A young man hits me up for a fiver,
says he wants to finish his graphic novel.
Are you going to get high? I ask.
No man, he says, *I'm done with that shit.
I want to be somebody.* I give him five bucks
and wish him good luck.

At 19th Street I walk down the steps, cross
10th Avenue and become again that little boy
standing in front of the bar, listening
to the noisy trains lumber along the tracks.
How many times, how many times do I look
through the window and imagine her sipping
her highball? Mother, I whisper, my breath
fogging the pane of cold glass,
> *I could use some help.*
> *I want to be somebody.*

Past Time

I must've nodded off before lifting from Heathrow,
when startled by Rachmaninoff, I realize that grief and relief
rhyme. I am listening to the Second Piano Concerto, featured
in more than forty films, each of which has made me cry.

I never liked Rachmaninoff. Too schmaltzy, I thought.
Too much with the strings. Now I love the schmaltz.
I love the strings. I dwell in a city called nostalgia
where no one I know is alive.

In the aisle attendants demonstrate how to buckle the belt
we've already buckled, then the vest. Should the unimaginable
happen, I imagine I'll strap it on backwards and bounce
down the inflatable slide to the bottom of the frigid Atlantic.

Last night at St. Martin-in-the-Fields I stepped over the graves
in the crypt, then sat under a translucent crucifix and listened
to the First String Quartet by Grieg. He wrote to a friend,
It strives towards breadth and soaring flight.

As the ensemble tricked the strings of their instruments
into their beautiful screaming, I thought of my father
who made enemies die during the war, and when it was over,
changed out of his blue collar each week, and put on a suit
to listen to the Philharmonic.

What my father wanted was rarely the same as what he got.
He wanted me to believe I was born on the only day in history
when nothing else happened. He wanted me to love
his music and thought he'd failed.

Grand Fugue

After the hospital released me with a warning,
I walked around this busy city that hadn't noticed
I'd been missing, me and my reconstructed heart,
so full of gratitude I wanted to kiss every light
that flashed GO, forgive the ones that said STOP.
And when I felt the earth throb under my feet,
I remembered the subway below where commuters
were training themselves to work and what it felt
like to be that useful, which I will never be again
until my living will kicks in and a young doctor-to-be
pulls out my organs, examines them, and puts them back,
leaving one out to see if anyone notices, the way I did
in boot camp after taking an ancient carbine apart,
getting busted, threatened with court martial and firing
squad and Vietnam. The sun is working overtime,
shimmying its Vitamin D all over the city. Its light
reflects off the granite walls of a magnificent building
whose cornerstone says it was born in 1844,
the year nitrous oxide was first used to sweeten pain,
though too late for Beethoven, who, enraged after
becoming deaf, drove the audience mad when he came
up with his fifteen-minute car crash, the "Grosse Fugue,"
where the violin and the two violas and the cello
rip their bows across the screaming catgut
so atonally, no one wanted to listen to it.
Wouldn't his heart break from joy if a patron set him up
at Weeki Wachee to watch through the great glass wall,
mermaids breathing underwater from air hoses so obvious

you can't see them? His whole universe would shimmer
as waterproof women swirl through the bubbles
of the sunlit spring, smiling at him, waving their colorful
spandex tails like batons. In my anesthetic dreams,
I too breathe underwater without drowning.
I flap my arms, kick my feet, try not to remember
how blood spilling out of the body congeals
on the hospital sheets so a minimum wage worker
in the basement laundry can put a Whopper and fries
on her kid's dinner plate. There are a million birds
in this city I hadn't heard till now, each of them tuning
their instruments, each of them singing, I am alive.

Stars Poetica

The first thing you notice is how
lonely they are, how what they desire
consumes them. Who knows how long
their longing lasts? They come from dust,
like us, and to dust they will return.
Forget what you were told
about their *twinkling*. When their
magnificent voices begin to trill,
their songs flicker. Love, after all,
attracts dust to dust, flame to flame.
Who knows what a second means
to them? A century? Whatever questions
you may have, you should know,
they have the same questions.

Of course when they wish, they do not wish
upon themselves. But they do wish
to be held, knowing nothing can hold them.
To be held means to be *restrained*
or *consoled*. Like Boethius awaiting execution
in a cell in Pavia, he consoled himself
composing his song, *O happy race
of mortals, if your hearts are ruled,
as is the universe, by love.* Our love,
both too soft and too loud, is more than love.
And dust is more than dust. As you wipe
it from the credenza, as you brush it
with your hand from your lapel, you must
never forget, you too were once on fire.

Acknowledgments

My gratitude to the hardworking editors of the following publications where some of these poems made their debut.

Atlanta Review: "In Wild Matrimony"
Coastal Forest Review: "Between Earth and Heaven"
Commonweal: "Art Song," "Eclipse," "The Forgotten Man," "Miss Besieged Sarajevo," "The Payload"
Diode Poetry Journal: "Stars Poetica"
The Houston Literary Review: "Death and the Miser"
Laurel Review: "The Duality of Dust"
The Ledge: "Benediction"
Light: A Journal of Poetry and Photography: "Closing Time," "Past Time"
The Literary Review: "Aspirin"
The Little Magazine: "House Angels"
Mead: "Glass Box," "Schooled"
New York Quarterly: "The Book of Stars"
Ozone Park: "Restraint"
Passager: "Spontaneous Combustion"
Philadelphia Stories: "The Hunger of Tides"
Poetry City: "Erased"
Poetry Wales: "Bad History"
Rattle: "Grand Fugue"
Rhino: "The Boy in the Tree"
Santa Clara Review: "Prostitutes Appeal to Pope"
Scapegoat Review: "Good Boy," "Home"
Sleet Magazine: "Local Birds," "Stairs to All Levels"
Solstice: A Magazine of Diverse Voices: "This Time"

The Somerset Review: "The Resentment of Stars"
Tiferet Journal: "The God Nobody Wanted," "Mulk (Dominion)," "Rahmat (Mercy)"
Typehouse: "The Diaspora of Light"
U.S. 1 Worksheets: "Birthday," "The Business of Clouds," "Hunger"
Washington Square: "Rush Hour"
Zymergy: "On Pain and Desire"

"Art Song," "Eclipse," "The Forgotten Man," "Miss Besieged Sarajevo," and "The Payload" are reprinted with the permission of *Commonweal Magazine.*

"The Free Market" was published in *Transition: Poems in the Aftermath,* ed. Michael Broder (Indolent Press, 2018).

"The Fury of Bananas" was published in the *2020 Anthology of Featured Poets,* ed. Larry Robins (Moonstone Press, 2021).

"Closing Time" was reprinted in *The First Wave,* eds. Wendy Kaplan and Toni Libro (Beach Bards Poetry & Prose Reading Series, 2020).

"Grand Fugue" was reprinted in *NJ Poets, Palisades, Parkways & Pinelands,* ed. Gregg G. Brown (Blast Press, 2016).

"House Angels" was reprinted in *What the House Knows,* ed. Diane Lockward (Terrapin Books, 2025).

"In Wild Matrimony" was reprinted in *Atlanta Review 10th Anniversary Anthology,* ed. Dan Veach (*Atlanta Review*, 2005).

"This Time" was reprinted in *Welcome to the Resistance: Poetry as Protest,* ed. Taylor Carman Savath (South Jersey Culture & History Center, Stockton University, 2021).

"Grand Fugue," "Local Birds" and "The God Nobody Wanted" appeared in *I Thought I Was Going to Be Okay,* a limited edition chapbook (Diode Editions, 2016).

"Closing Time," "Past Time," and "This Time" appeared in *Mean Time,* a limited edition chapbook (Moonstone Press, 2019).

Thanks, as always, to my wife Sonya for her patience, love, and ability to keep me sane, and to my daughter and best friend, Amanda, a bright, brilliant star blazing at the center of the universe.

About the Author

Peter E. Murphy was born in Wales and grew up in New York City. He is the author of a dozen previous books and chapbooks of poetry and prose, including *A Tipsy Fairy Tale: A Coming of Age Memoir of Alcohol and Redemption*. His writing has appeared in *Michigan Quarterly Review*, *New Welsh Reader*, *North American Review*, *The Sun*, and elsewhere. His honors include six fellowships from the New Jersey State Council on the Arts and residencies at Yaddo, the Atlantic Center for the Arts, and the Millay Colony. He has been a consultant to the Geraldine R. Dodge Foundation, the New Jersey State Council on the Arts, the New Jersey Council for the Humanities, and numerous school districts around the country. In addition, he has been an educational advisor to three PBS television programs on poetry produced by Bill Moyers. He is the founder of Murphy Writing of Stockton University in Atlantic City.

www.ingramcontent.com/pod-product-compliance
Lightning Source LLC
Chambersburg PA
CBHW030530080526
44586CB00011B/385